SOCCER
COACH
NOTEBOOK

NAME
_____

CLUB
_____

TEAM
_____

CONTACT
_____

SEASON
_____

OTHER INFO
_____

BOOQOOZE
booqooze.com

THIS BOOK INCLUDES FREE BONUS PAGES THAT ARE
AVAILABLE ON THE LAST PAGES

QR Code Website

Email
info@booqooze.com

ANNUAL PLANNER

JANUARY

FEBRUARY

MARCH

APRIL

MAY

JUNE

JULY

AUGUST

SEPTEMBER

OCTOBER

NOVEMBER

DECEMBER

IMPORTANT

NOTES

ATTENDANCE

PLAYERS

DATE

DATE

POS	LEAGUE TABLE	TEAM		P	W	D	L	PTS

MATCHES	DATE	TIME	SCORE	PTS

DATE	TIME	LOCATION/FIELD		
			HOME	AWAY
	OPPONENTS		HALF SCORE	FINAL SCORE

POS/NUM	PLAYER'S NAME	SUBSTIT. 1 T.	SUBSTIT. 2 T	NOTES / RATING
1 GOALKEEPER				

BEST PERFORMANCE	MATCH GOAL	MATCH GOAL	COACH'S NOTE

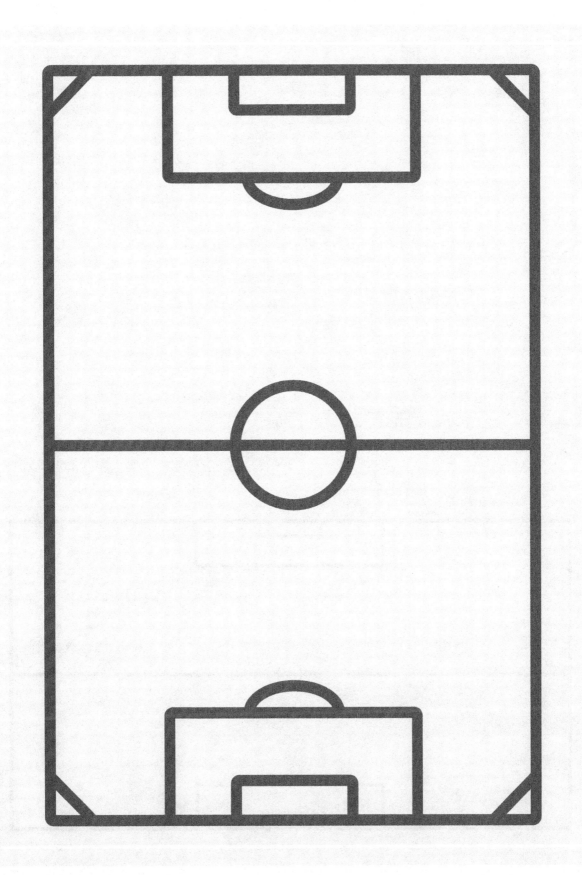

DATE	TIME		LOCATION/FIELD			

				HOME	AWAY
	OPPONENTS			HALF SCORE	FINAL SCORE

POS/NUM	PLAYER'S NAME	SUBSTIT. 1 T.	SUBSTIT. 2 T	NOTES / RATING
1 GOALKEEPER				

BEST PERFORMANCE	MATCH GOAL	MATCH GOAL	COACH'S NOTE

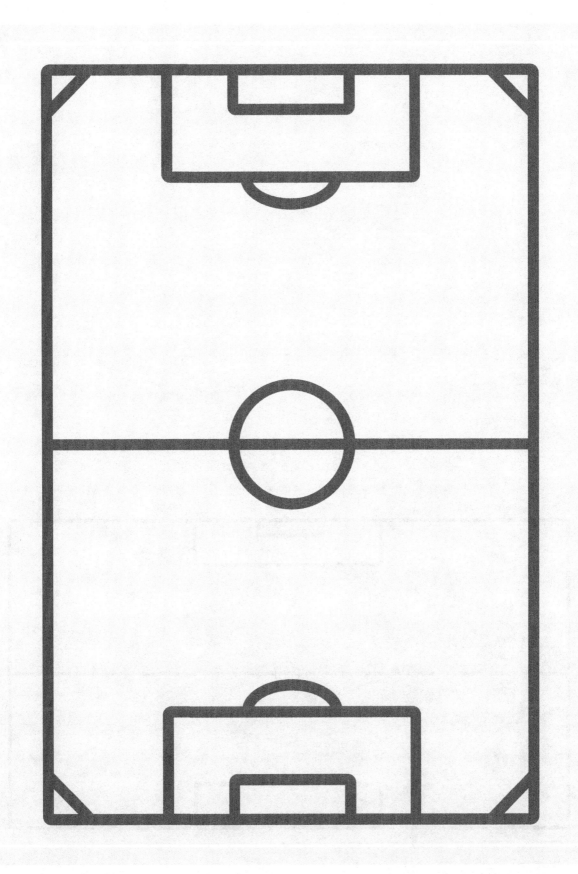

DATE	TIME		LOCATION/FIELD			

				HOME	AWAY
	OPPONENTS			HALF SCORE	FINAL SCORE

POS/NUM	PLAYER'S NAME	SUBSTIT. 1 T.	SUBSTIT. 2 T	NOTES / RATING
1 GOALKEEPER				

BEST PERFORMANCE	MATCH GOAL	MATCH GOAL	COACH'S NOTE

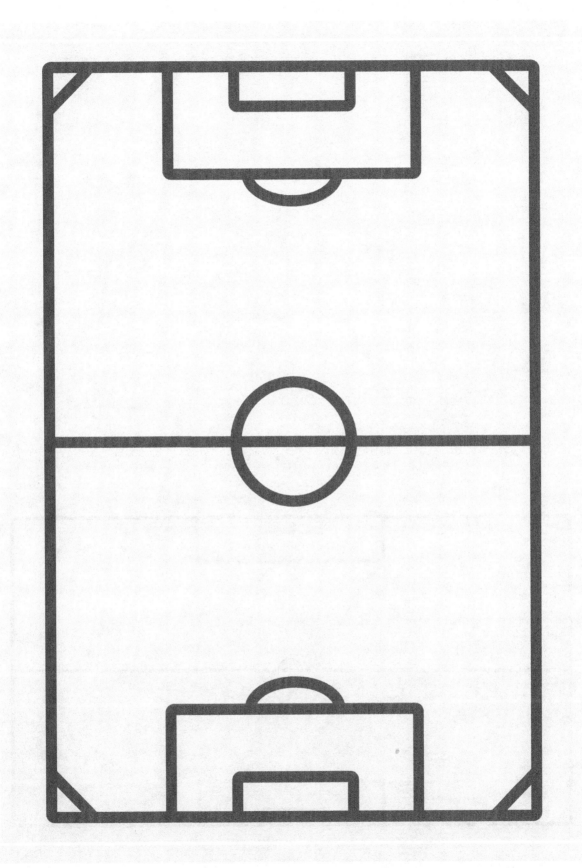

POS/NUM	PLAYER'S NAME	SUBSTIT. 1 T.	SUBSTIT. 2 T	NOTES / RATING
1 GOALKEEPER				

DATE   TIME   LOCATION/FIELD

HOME   AWAY

OPPONENTS   HALF SCORE   FINAL SCORE

BEST PERFORMANCE   MATCH GOAL   MATCH GOAL   COACH'S NOTE

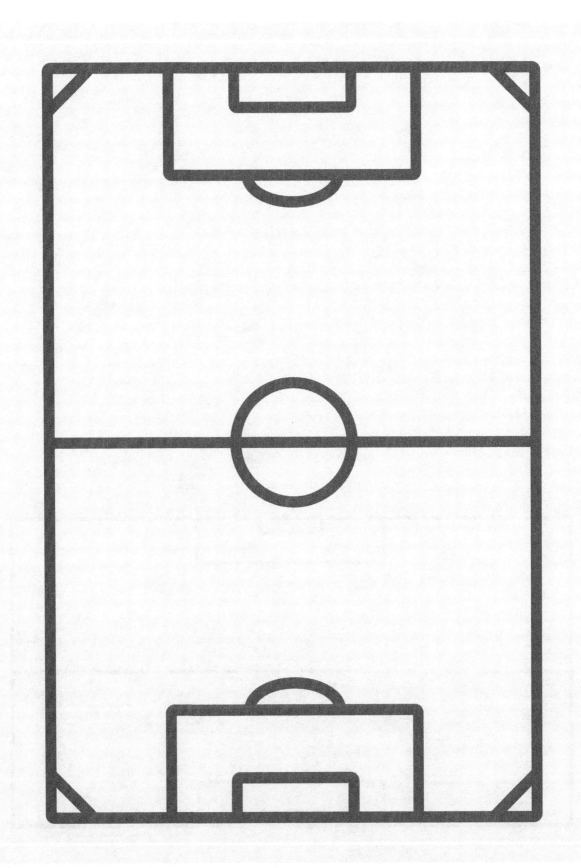

DATE	TIME	LOCATION/FIELD		
			HOME	AWAY
	OPPONENTS		HALF SCORE	FINAL SCORE

POS/NUM	PLAYER'S NAME	SUBSTIT. 1 T.	SUBSTIT. 2 T	NOTES / RATING
1 GOALKEEPER				

BEST PERFORMANCE	MATCH GOAL	MATCH GOAL	COACH'S NOTE

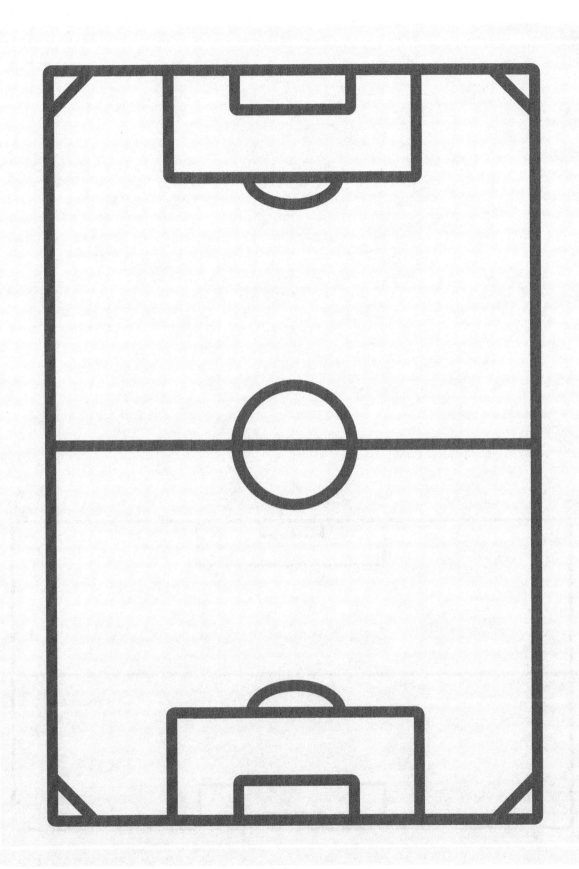

DATE	TIME		LOCATION/FIELD				

					HOME	AWAY
	OPPONENTS				HALF SCORE	FINAL SCORE

POS/NUM	PLAYER'S NAME	SUBSTIT. 1 T.	SUBSTIT. 2 T	NOTES / RATING
1 GOALKEEPER				

BEST PERFORMANCE	MATCH GOAL	MATCH GOAL	COACH'S NOTE

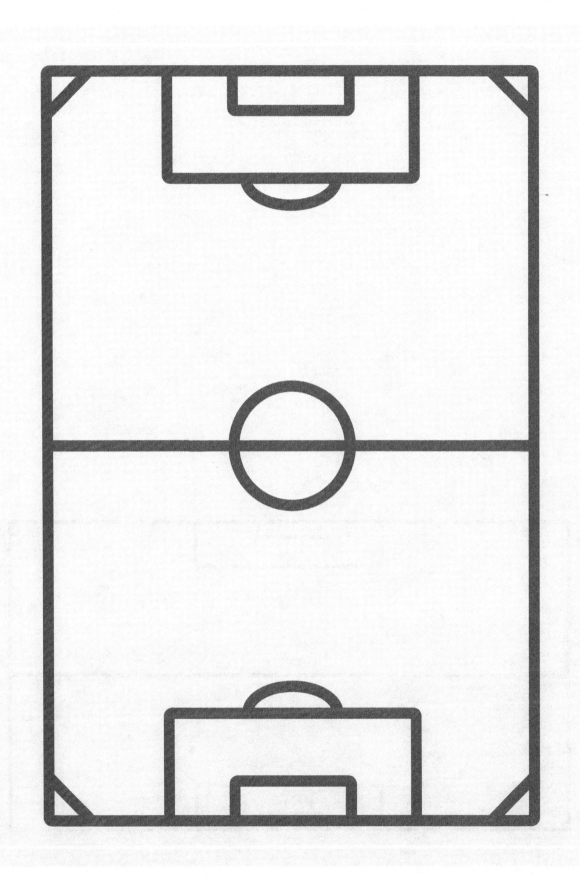

DATE	TIME		LOCATION/FIELD			

					HOME	AWAY
	OPPONENTS				HALF SCORE	FINAL SCORE

POS/NUM	PLAYER'S NAME	SUBSTIT. 1 T.	SUBSTIT. 2 T	NOTES / RATING
1 GOALKEEPER				

BEST PERFORMANCE	MATCH GOAL	MATCH GOAL	COACH'S NOTE

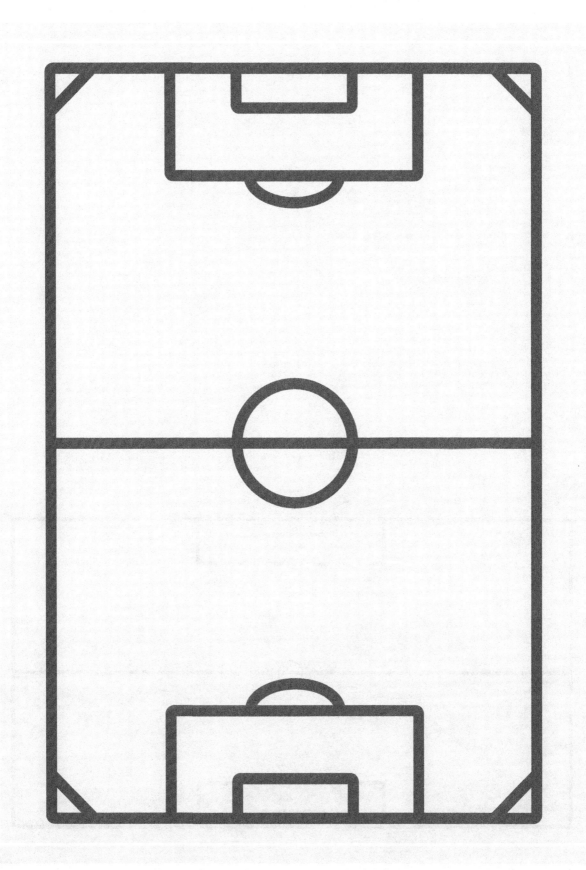

DATE	TIME	LOCATION/FIELD		
			HOME	AWAY
	OPPONENTS		HALF SCORE	FINAL SCORE

POS/NUM	PLAYER'S NAME	SUBSTIT. 1 T.	SUBSTIT. 2 T	NOTES / RATING
1 GOALKEEPER				

BEST PERFORMANCE	MATCH GOAL	MATCH GOAL	COACH'S NOTE

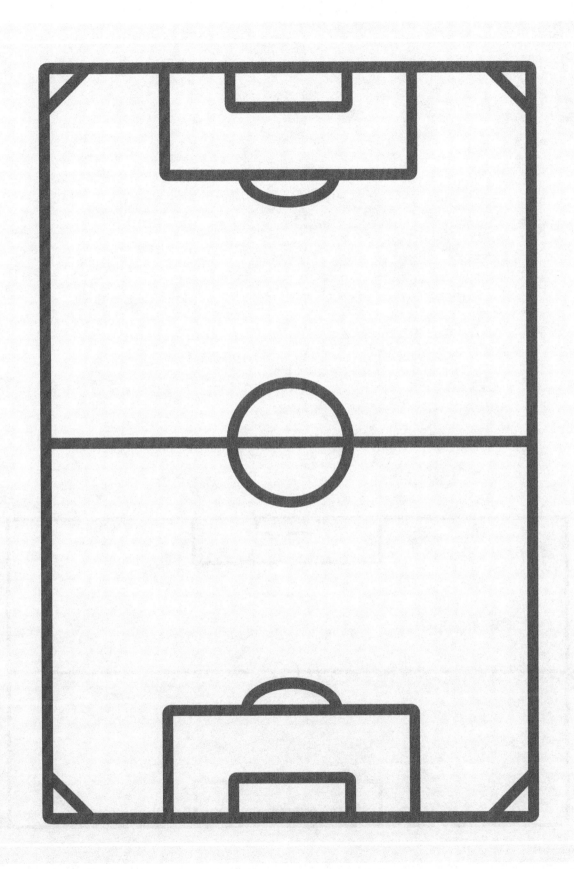

DATE	TIME		LOCATION/FIELD				
					HOME	AWAY	
		OPPONENTS			HALF SCORE	FINAL SCORE	

POS/NUM	PLAYER'S NAME	SUBSTIT. 1 T.	SUBSTIT. 2 T	NOTES / RATING
1 GOALKEEPER				

BEST PERFORMANCE	MATCH GOAL	MATCH GOAL	COACH'S NOTE

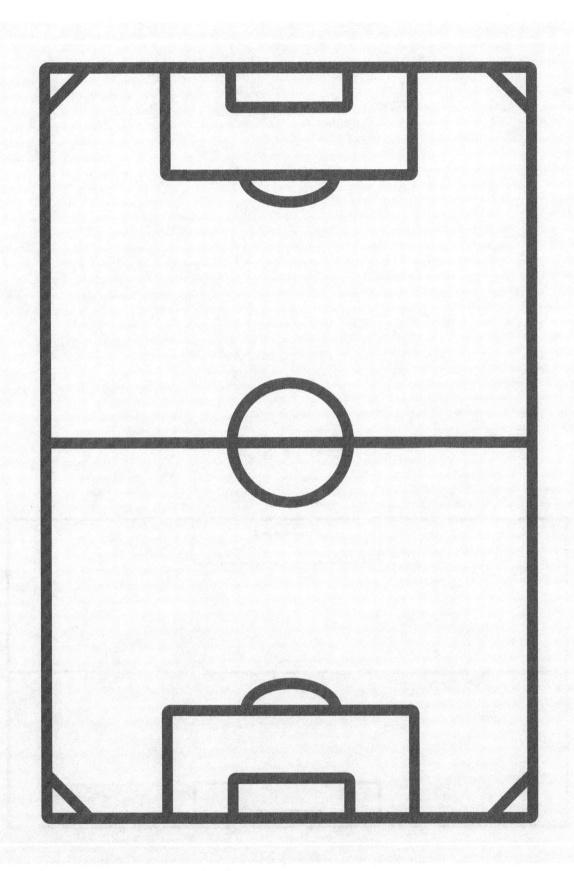

DATE	TIME	LOCATION/FIELD		

				HOME	AWAY
	OPPONENTS			HALF SCORE	FINAL SCORE

POS/NUM	PLAYER'S NAME	SUBSTIT. 1 T.	SUBSTIT. 2 T	NOTES / RATING
1 GOALKEEPER				

BEST PERFORMANCE	MATCH GOAL	MATCH GOAL	COACH'S NOTE

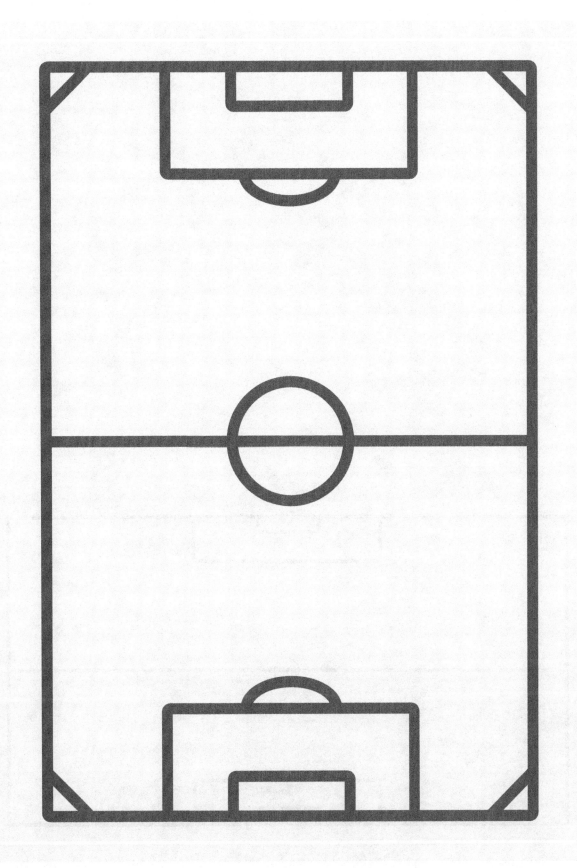

DATE	TIME		LOCATION/FIELD				
						HOME	AWAY
	OPPONENTS				HALF SCORE		FINAL SCORE

POS/NUM	PLAYER'S NAME	SUBSTIT. 1 T.	SUBSTIT. 2 T	NOTES / RATING
1 GOALKEEPER				

BEST PERFORMANCE	MATCH GOAL	MATCH GOAL	COACH'S NOTE

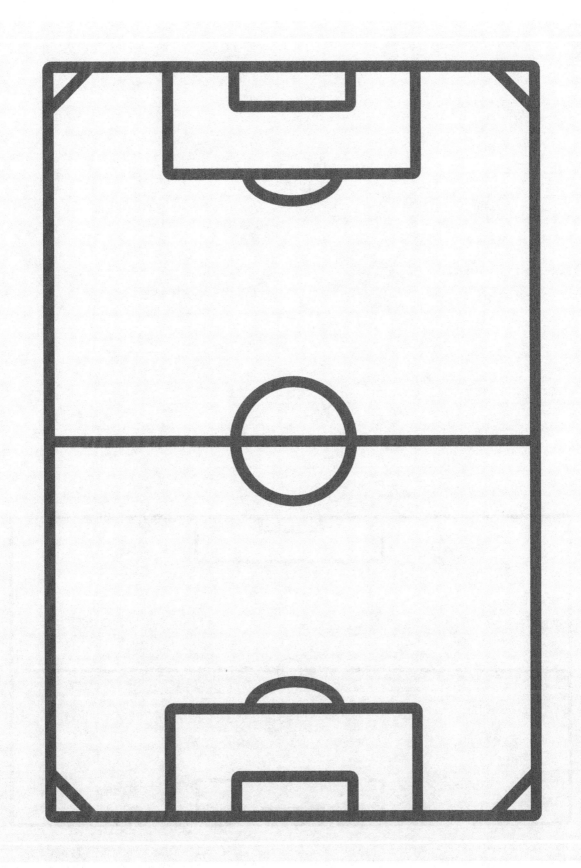

POS/NUM	PLAYER'S NAME	SUBSTIT. 1 T.	SUBSTIT. 2 T	NOTES / RATING
DATE	TIME		LOCATION/FIELD	

HOME AWAY

OPPONENTS HALF SCORE FINAL SCORE

POS/NUM	PLAYER'S NAME	SUBSTIT. 1 T.	SUBSTIT. 2 T	NOTES / RATING
1 GOALKEEPER				

BEST PERFORMANCE MATCH GOAL MATCH GOAL COACH'S NOTE

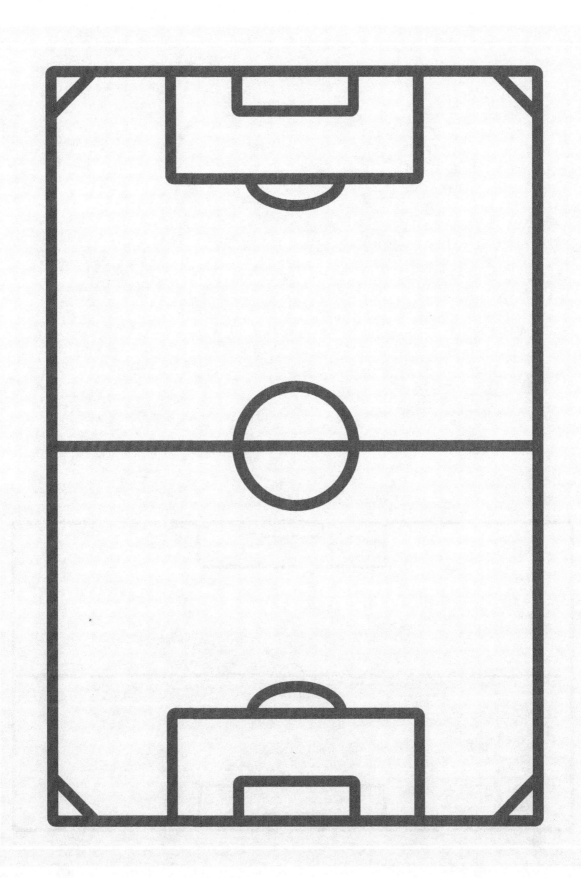

TRAINING SESSION / PRE-MATCH

DATE	TIME		LOCATION/FIELD				

					HOME	AWAY
	OPPONENTS				HALF SCORE	FINAL SCORE

POS/NUM	PLAYER'S NAME	SUBSTIT. 1 T.	SUBSTIT. 2 T	NOTES / RATING
1 GOALKEEPER				

BEST PERFORMANCE	MATCH GOAL	MATCH GOAL	COACH'S NOTE

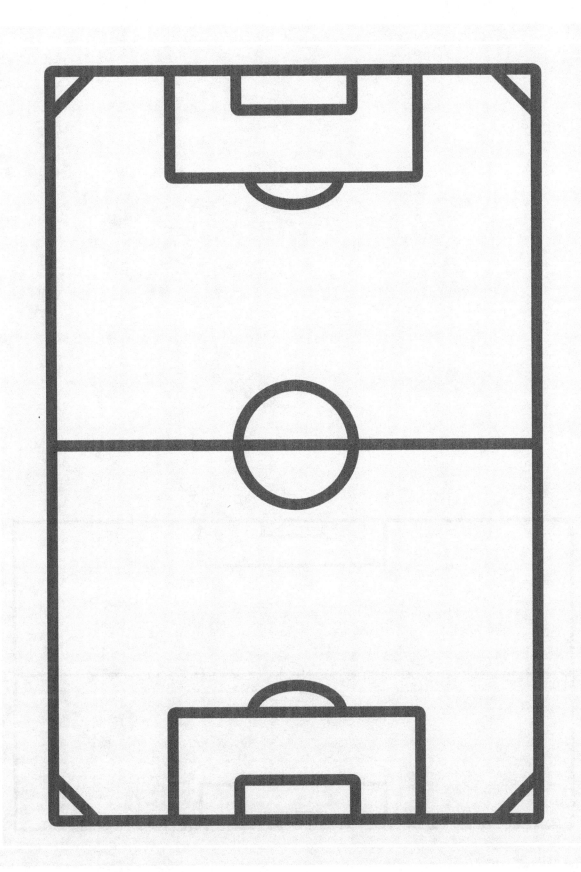

DATE	TIME	LOCATION/FIELD			
				HOME	AWAY
	OPPONENTS		HALF SCORE	FINAL SCORE	

POS/NUM	PLAYER'S NAME	SUBSTIT. 1 T.	SUBSTIT. 2 T	NOTES / RATING
1 GOALKEEPER				

BEST PERFORMANCE	MATCH GOAL	MATCH GOAL	COACH'S NOTE

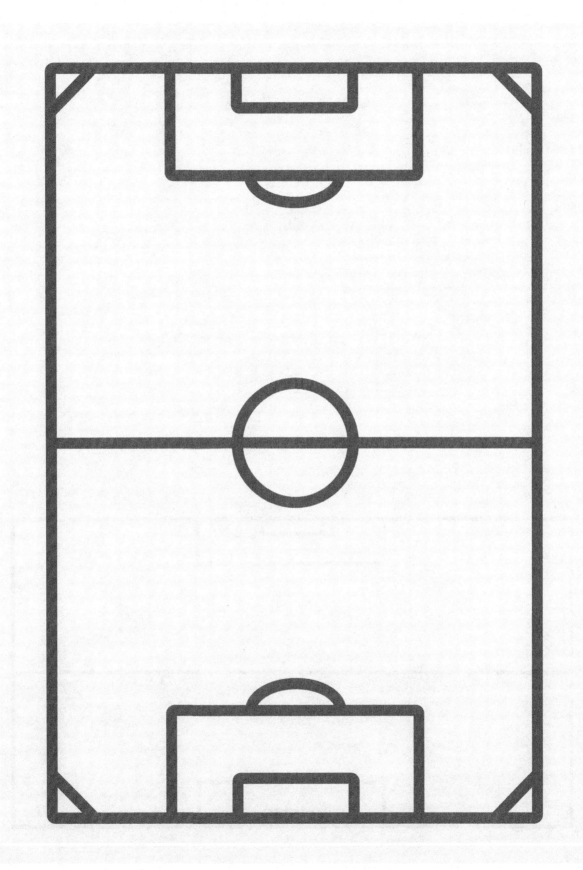

DATE	TIME		LOCATION/FIELD			
					HOME	AWAY
		OPPONENTS			HALF SCORE	FINAL SCORE

POS/NUM	PLAYER'S NAME	SUBSTIT. 1 T.	SUBSTIT. 2 T	NOTES / RATING
1 GOALKEEPER				

BEST PERFORMANCE	MATCH GOAL	MATCH GOAL	COACH'S NOTE

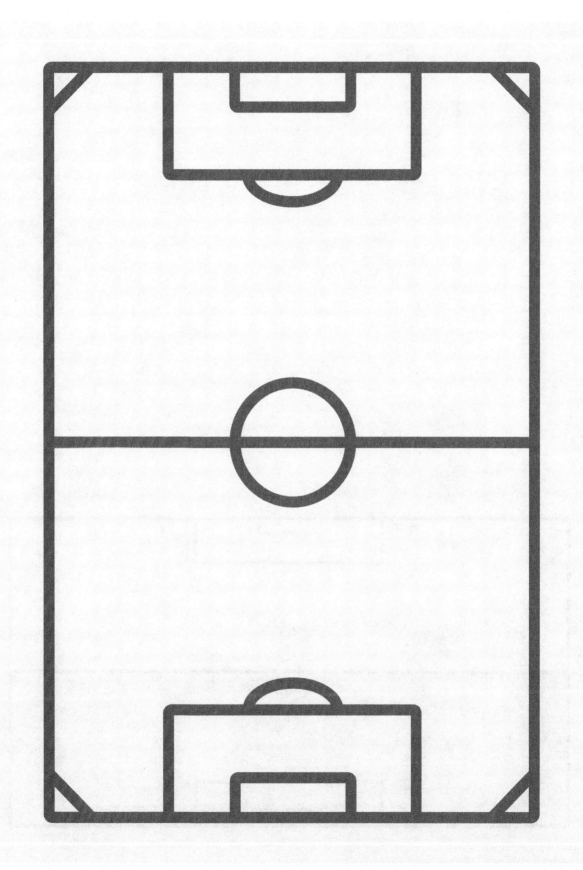

DATE	TIME		LOCATION/FIELD			
					HOME	AWAY
		OPPONENTS			HALF SCORE	FINAL SCORE

POS/NUM	PLAYER'S NAME	SUBSTIT. 1 T.	SUBSTIT. 2 T	NOTES / RATING
1 GOALKEEPER				

BEST PERFORMANCE	MATCH GOAL	MATCH GOAL	COACH'S NOTE

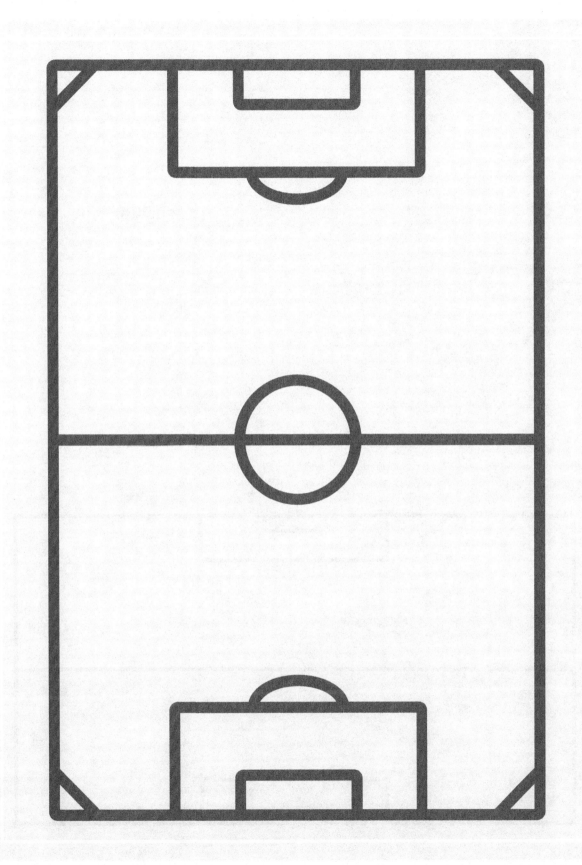

POS/NUM	PLAYER'S NAME	SUBSTIT. 1 T.	SUBSTIT. 2 T	NOTES / RATING
1 GOALKEEPER				

DATE   TIME   LOCATION/FIELD

HOME   AWAY

OPPONENTS   HALF SCORE   FINAL SCORE

BEST PERFORMANCE   MATCH GOAL   MATCH GOAL   COACH'S NOTE

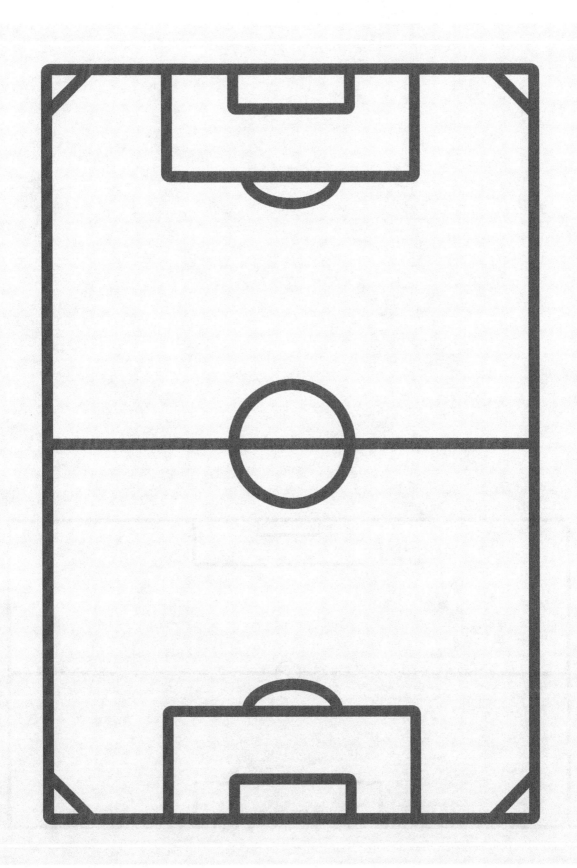

DATE	TIME		LOCATION/FIELD			

					HOME	AWAY
	OPPONENTS				HALF SCORE	FINAL SCORE

POS/NUM	PLAYER'S NAME	SUBSTIT. 1 T.	SUBSTIT. 2 T	NOTES / RATING
1 GOALKEEPER				

BEST PERFORMANCE	MATCH GOAL	MATCH GOAL	COACH'S NOTE

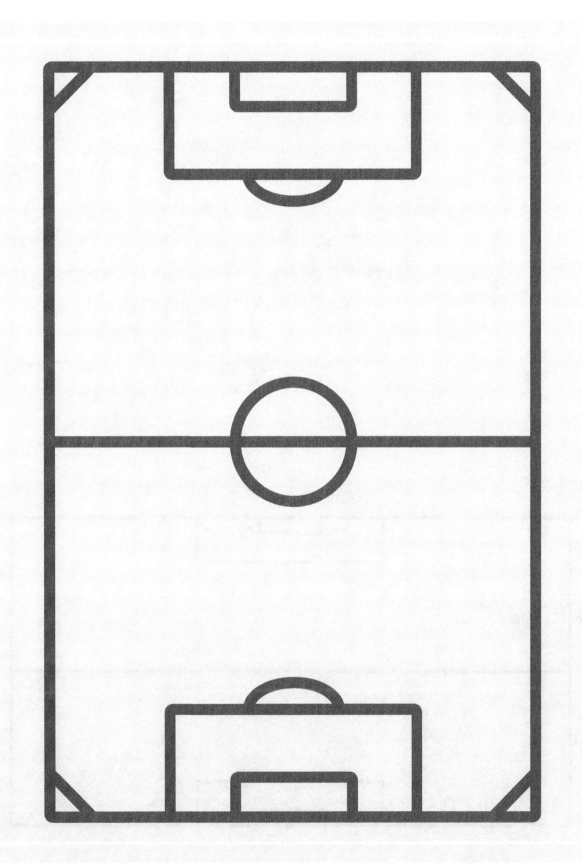

DATE	TIME		LOCATION/FIELD				

					HOME	AWAY
	OPPONENTS				HALF SCORE	FINAL SCORE

POS/NUM	PLAYER'S NAME	SUBSTIT. 1 T.	SUBSTIT. 2 T	NOTES / RATING
1 GOALKEEPER				

BEST PERFORMANCE	MATCH GOAL	MATCH GOAL	COACH'S NOTE

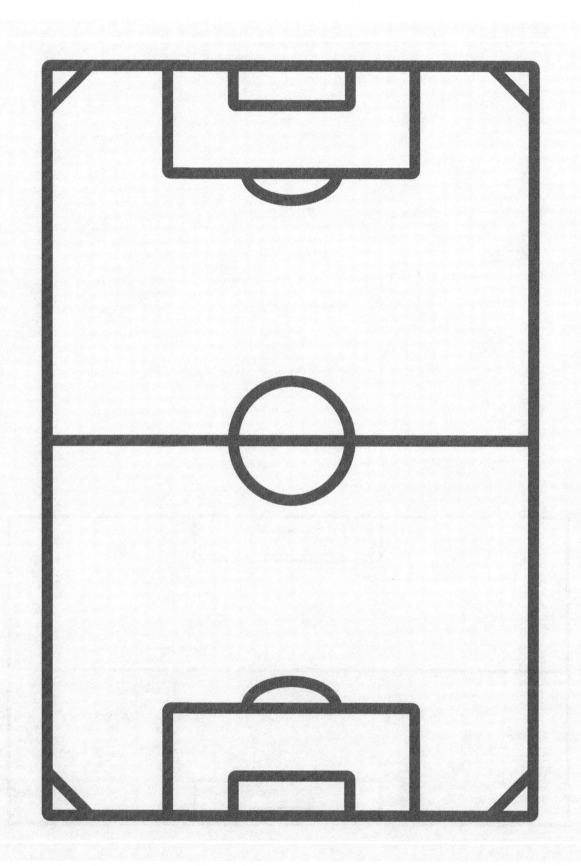

DATE	TIME	LOCATION/FIELD		
			HOME	AWAY
	OPPONENTS		HALF SCORE	FINAL SCORE

POS/NUM	PLAYER'S NAME	SUBSTIT. 1 T.	SUBSTIT. 2 T	NOTES / RATING
1 GOALKEEPER				

BEST PERFORMANCE	MATCH GOAL	MATCH GOAL	COACH'S NOTE

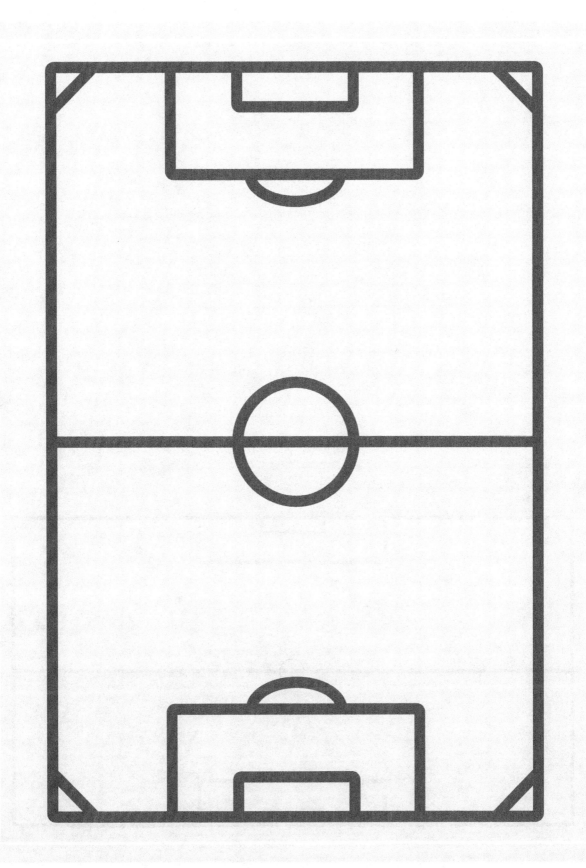

POS/NUM	PLAYER'S NAME	SUBSTIT. 1 T.	SUBSTIT. 2 T	NOTES / RATING
1 GOALKEEPER				

DATE   TIME   LOCATION/FIELD

HOME   AWAY

OPPONENTS   HALF SCORE   FINAL SCORE

BEST PERFORMANCE   MATCH GOAL   MATCH GOAL   COACH'S NOTE

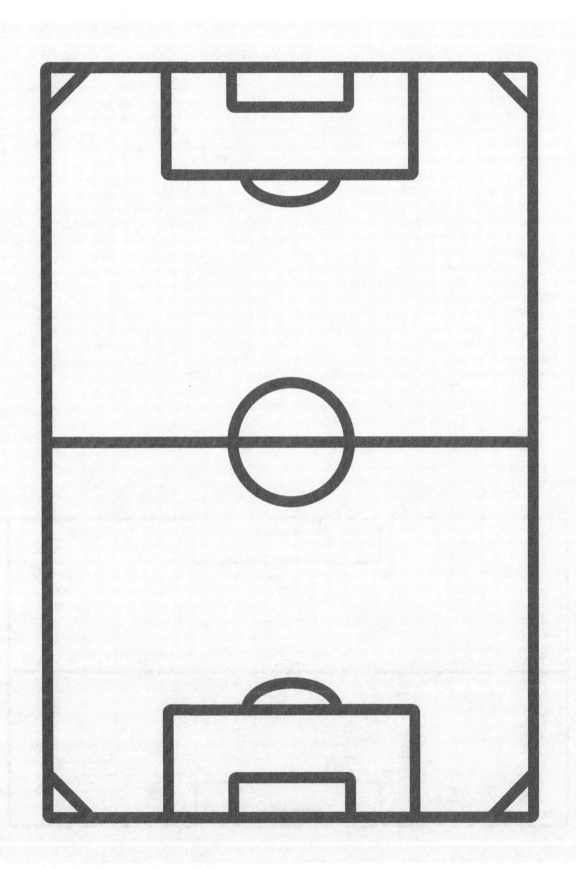

POS/NUM	PLAYER'S NAME	SUBSTIT. 1 T.	SUBSTIT. 2 T	NOTES / RATING
DATE	TIME		LOCATION/FIELD	

HOME   AWAY

OPPONENTS   HALF SCORE   FINAL SCORE

POS/NUM	PLAYER'S NAME	SUBSTIT. 1 T.	SUBSTIT. 2 T	NOTES / RATING
1 GOALKEEPER				

BEST PERFORMANCE	MATCH GOAL	MATCH GOAL	COACH'S NOTE

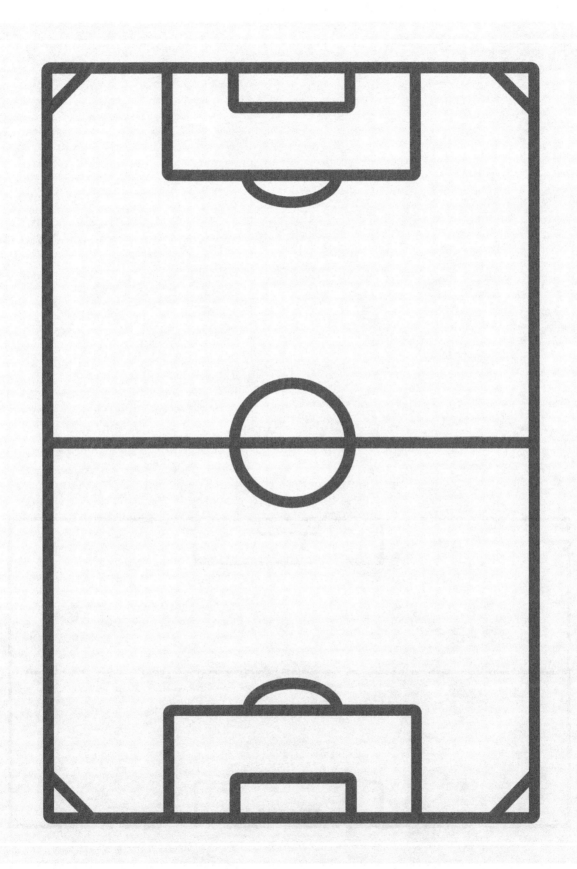

DATE	TIME	LOCATION/FIELD		
			HOME	AWAY
	OPPONENTS		HALF SCORE	FINAL SCORE

POS/NUM	PLAYER'S NAME	SUBSTIT. 1 T.	SUBSTIT. 2 T	NOTES / RATING
1 GOALKEEPER				

BEST PERFORMANCE	MATCH GOAL	MATCH GOAL	COACH'S NOTE

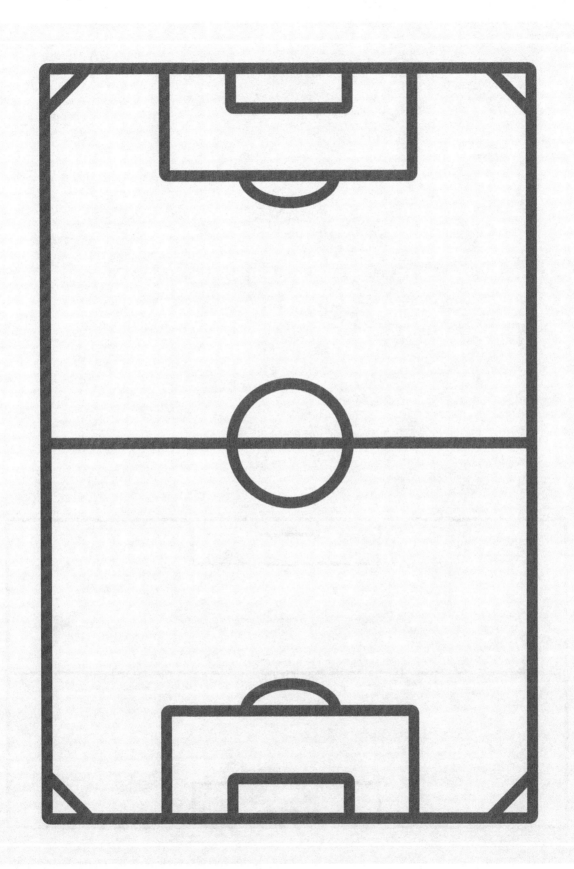

DATE	TIME		LOCATION/FIELD			
					HOME	AWAY
		OPPONENTS			HALF SCORE	FINAL SCORE

POS/NUM	PLAYER'S NAME	SUBSTIT. 1 T.	SUBSTIT. 2 T	NOTES / RATING
1 GOALKEEPER				

BEST PERFORMANCE	MATCH GOAL	MATCH GOAL	COACH'S NOTE

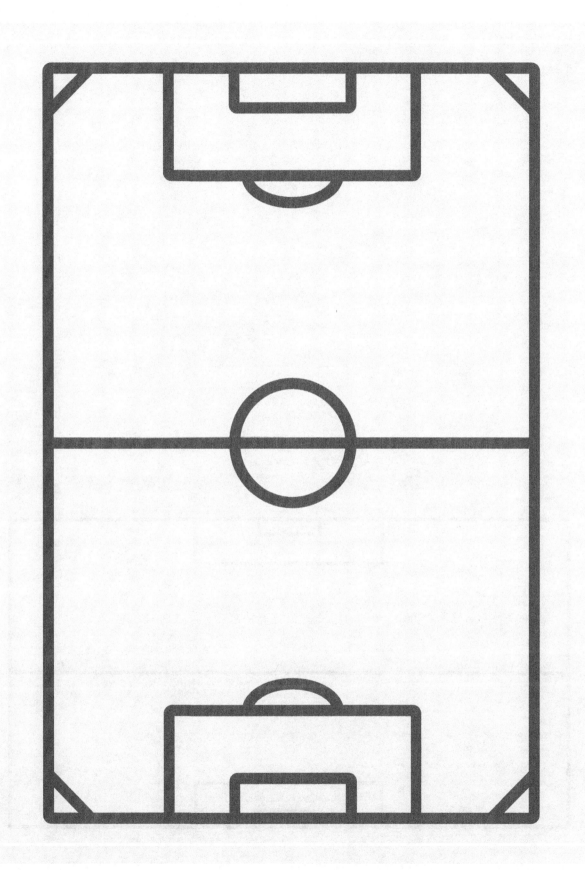

DATE	TIME	LOCATION/FIELD		
			HOME	AWAY
	OPPONENTS		HALF SCORE	FINAL SCORE

POS/NUM	PLAYER'S NAME	SUBSTIT. 1 T.	SUBSTIT. 2 T	NOTES / RATING
1 GOALKEEPER				

BEST PERFORMANCE	MATCH GOAL	MATCH GOAL	COACH'S NOTE

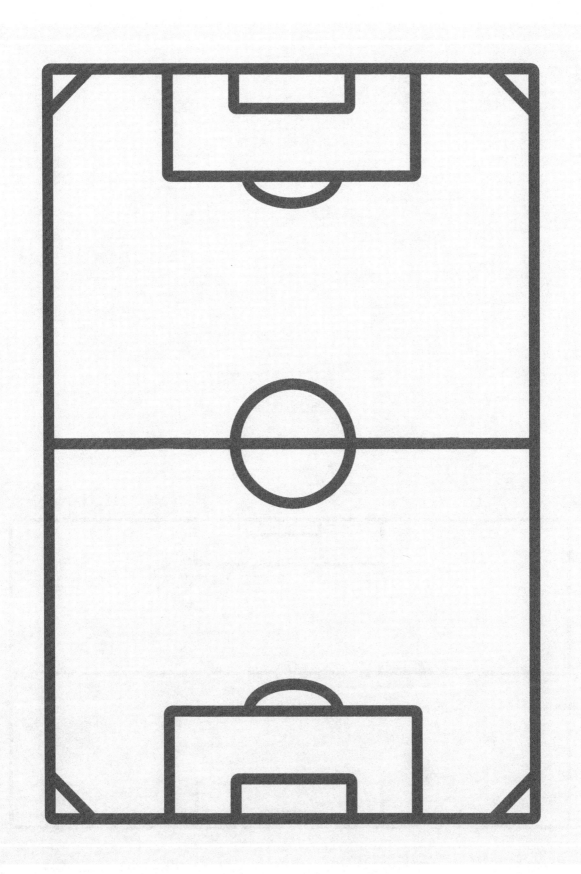

DATE	TIME	LOCATION/FIELD		
			HOME	AWAY
	OPPONENTS		HALF SCORE	FINAL SCORE

POS/NUM	PLAYER'S NAME	SUBSTIT. 1 T.	SUBSTIT. 2 T	NOTES / RATING
1 GOALKEEPER				

BEST PERFORMANCE	MATCH GOAL	MATCH GOAL	COACH'S NOTE

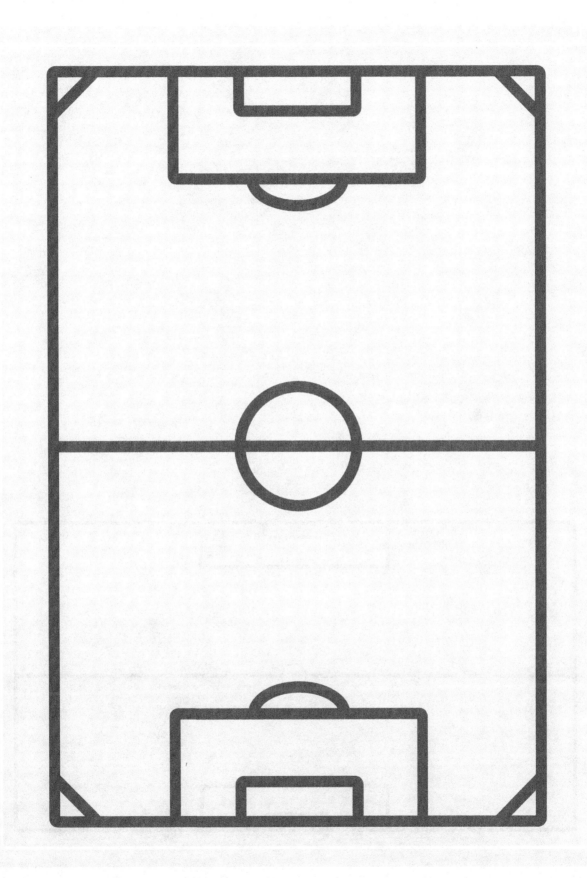

DATE	TIME		LOCATION/FIELD			
					HOME	AWAY
		OPPONENTS			HALF SCORE	FINAL SCORE

POS/NUM	PLAYER'S NAME	SUBSTIT. 1 T.	SUBSTIT. 2 T	NOTES / RATING
1 GOALKEEPER				

BEST PERFORMANCE	MATCH GOAL	MATCH GOAL	COACH'S NOTE

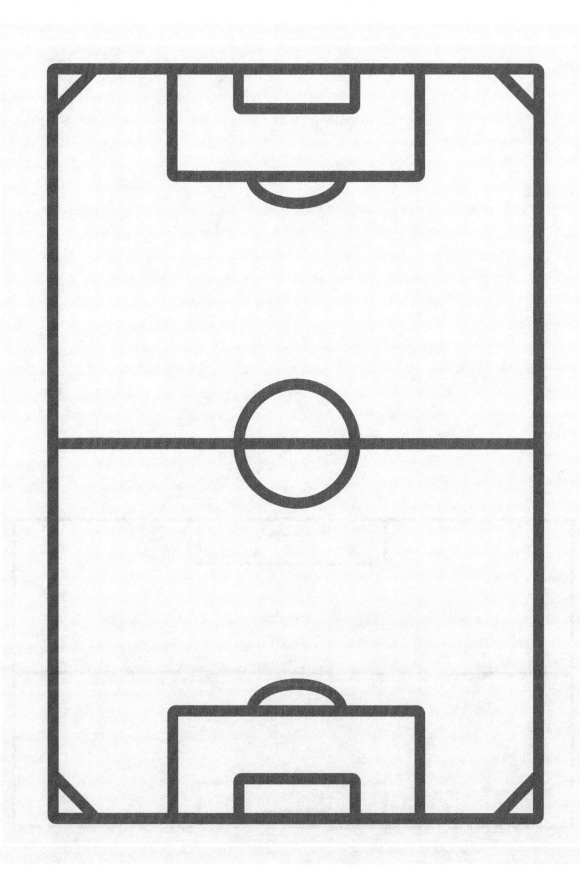

DATE	TIME	LOCATION/FIELD		

			HOME	AWAY
	OPPONENTS		HALF SCORE	FINAL SCORE

POS/NUM	PLAYER'S NAME	SUBSTIT. 1 T.	SUBSTIT. 2 T	NOTES / RATING
1 GOALKEEPER				

BEST PERFORMANCE	MATCH GOAL	MATCH GOAL	COACH'S NOTE

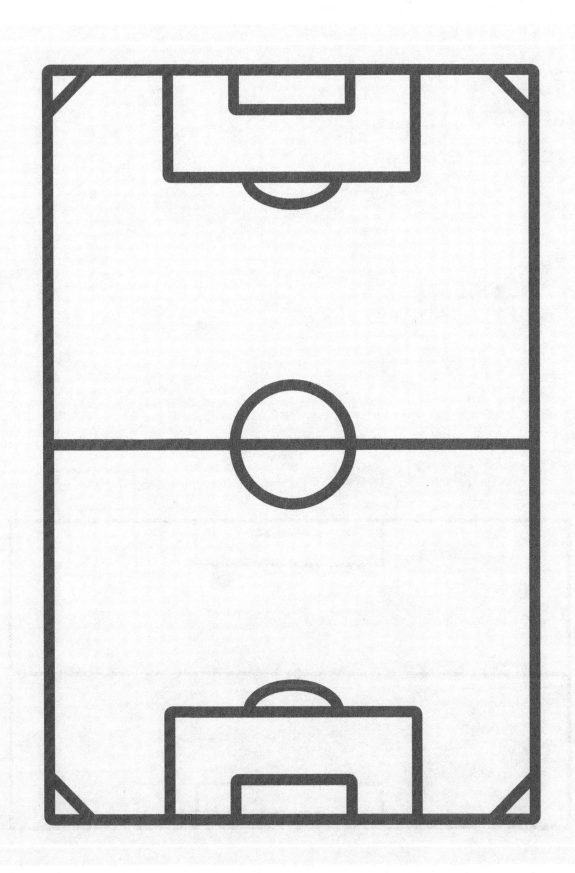

NOTES

POS/NUM	PLAYER'S NAME	SUBSTIT. 1 T.	SUBSTIT. 2 T	NOTES / RATING
1 GOALKEEPER				

DATE   TIME   LOCATION/FIELD

HOME   AWAY

OPPONENTS   HALF SCORE   FINAL SCORE

BEST PERFORMANCE   MATCH GOAL   MATCH GOAL   COACH'S NOTE

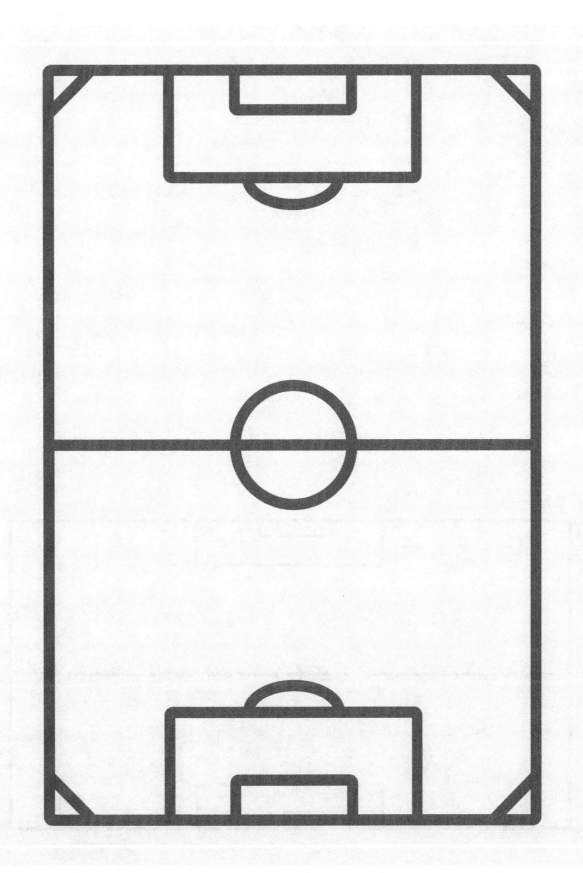

NOTES

DATE	TIME	LOCATION/FIELD			
				HOME	AWAY
	OPPONENTS			HALF SCORE	FINAL SCORE

POS/NUM	PLAYER'S NAME	SUBSTIT. 1 T.	SUBSTIT. 2 T	NOTES / RATING
1 GOALKEEPER				

BEST PERFORMANCE	MATCH GOAL	MATCH GOAL	COACH'S NOTE

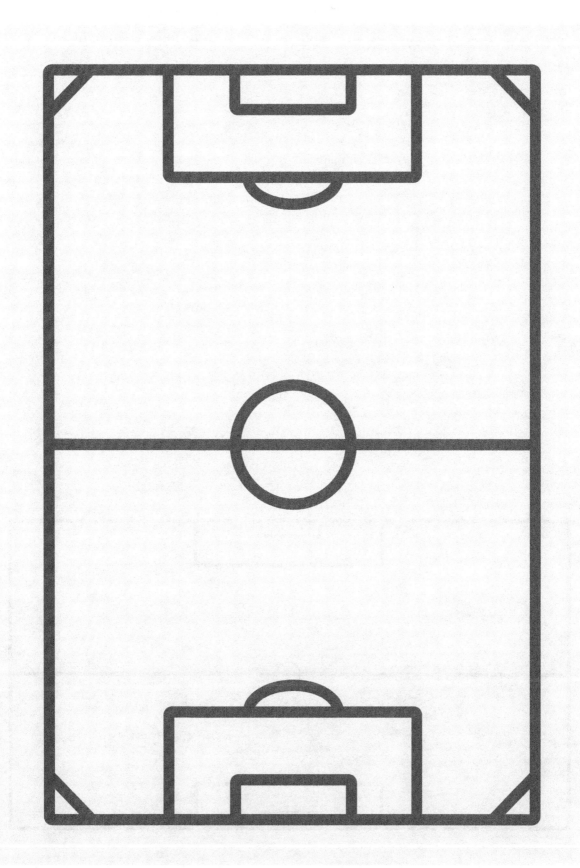

DATE	TIME		LOCATION/FIELD			
					HOME	AWAY
		OPPONENTS			HALF SCORE	FINAL SCORE

POS/NUM	PLAYER'S NAME	SUBSTIT. 1 T.	SUBSTIT. 2 T	NOTES / RATING
1 GOALKEEPER				

BEST PERFORMANCE	MATCH GOAL	MATCH GOAL	COACH'S NOTE

POS/NUM	PLAYER'S NAME	SUBSTIT. 1 T.	SUBSTIT. 2 T	NOTES / RATING

DATE **TIME** **LOCATION/FIELD**

HOME **AWAY**

OPPONENTS **HALF SCORE** **FINAL SCORE**

POS/NUM	PLAYER'S NAME	SUBSTIT. 1 T.	SUBSTIT. 2 T	NOTES / RATING
1 GOALKEEPER				

BEST PERFORMANCE **MATCH GOAL** **MATCH GOAL** **COACH'S NOTE**

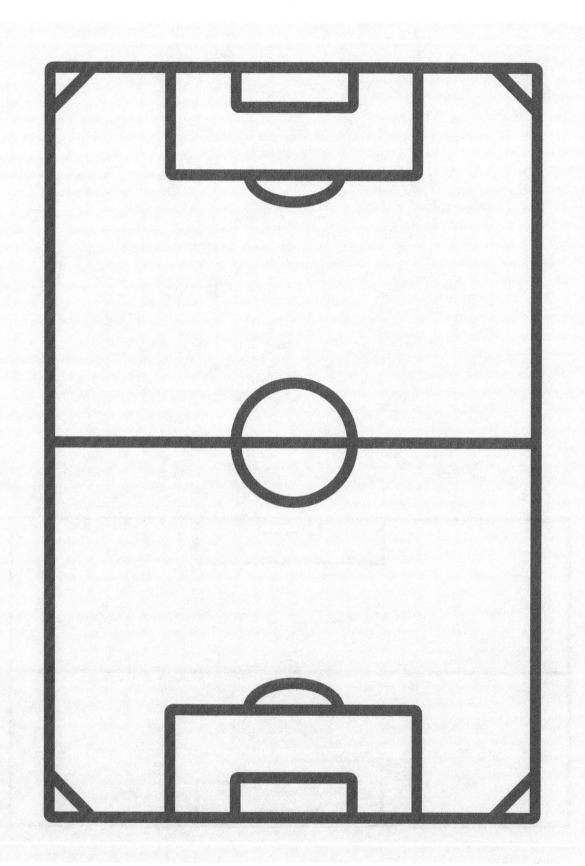

DATE	TIME	LOCATION/FIELD		
			HOME	AWAY
	OPPONENTS		HALF SCORE	FINAL SCORE

POS/NUM	PLAYER'S NAME	SUBSTIT. 1 T.	SUBSTIT. 2 T	NOTES / RATING
1 GOALKEEPER				

BEST PERFORMANCE	MATCH GOAL	MATCH GOAL	COACH'S NOTE

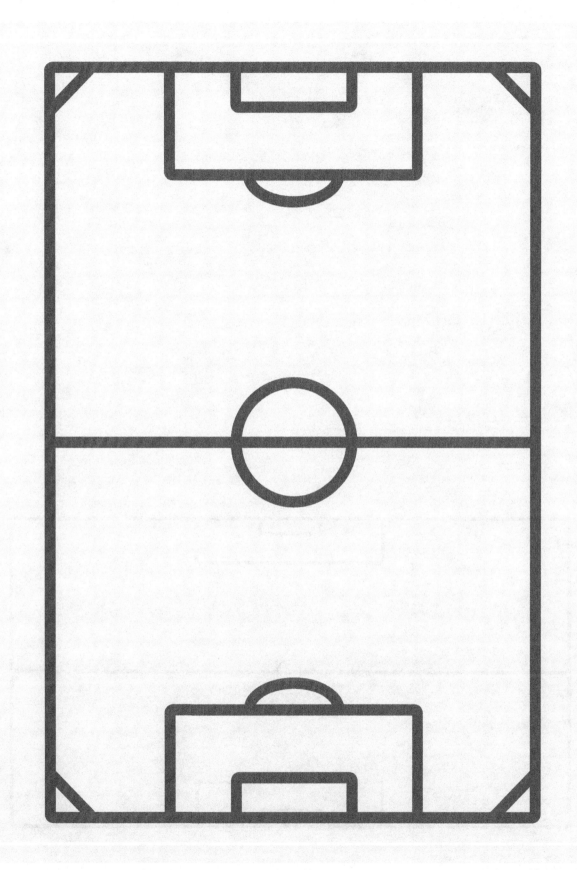

NOTE

NOTE

NOTE

- Bonus Page -

Dear Reader,
We thank you for choosing our
Logbook for soccer coaches.
To demonstrate our commitment
we have prepared free resources for you:

You will receive more than once various Templates that I hope
will serve you in your work as a Coach. I have divided these
free pages into several sections. You will receive templates
divided into these sections:

Player - Team - Template - Match

Vers. 1   Vers. 2   Vers. 3   Vers. 4

You will find 4 different Sections

Section
Player

Section
Team

Section
Match

Section
Template

But that's not all!

After receiving this set of free content,
You will have exclusive access to:

With this checklist you can better organise your training session, knowing exactly what and how much material you need to make your team stronger and more motivated.

Simply enter the quantities of the equipment you want to use for your activities, such as balls, cones, bibs, goals, etc., and this checklist will automatically calculate the total. This way, you can prepare the playground in advance, with all the equipment ready and placed in the right places. This will allow you to optimise your time, reducing breaks and increasing the intensity of your training.

BOOQOOZE

In this quiz, you will find 16 multiple choice questions on various aspects of football.

- For each question, you will have to choose the answer you think is most correct from the four options proposed.

- After you answer, I will tell you whether you guessed right or not, and give you an explanation and sources to further investigate the topic.

- At the end of the quiz, I will give you a score and personalised feedback on your coaching skills.

You can download the Pages here:
https://booqooze.com/special-content-football-soccer

You can download the Pages here:
https://booqooze.com/special-content-football-soccer

Thank you again for choosing our logbook.
Sincerely, Booqooze Team

- booqooze.com -

If our Logbook was helpful,
we invite you to leave a review on Amazon.
Reader reviews are extremely important to us and help us
reach a wider audience and share this essential information
with more people.

We personally check and evaluate each one simply to gather
additional feedback.

Here is a QR code that will take you directly to the Amazon
review npage without too many clicks:

https://b9g5.short.gy/MisterUsa

Greetings,
the Booqooze Team

*A warm greeting from
the entire Booqooze Team.*

Made in the USA
Monee, IL
21 March 2025